swimming and diving

robert sandelson

OLYMPIC SPORTS

Crestwood House
New York

Maxwell Macmillan International
New York   Oxford   Singapore   Sydney

TRACK ATHLETICS
FIELD ATHLETICS
SWIMMING AND DIVING
GYMNASTICS
ICE SPORTS
SKIING
BALL SPORTS
COMBAT SPORTS

Designer: Ian Roberts
Editor: Deborah Elliott

Cover: The 100-m breaststroke final at the 1984
Olympic Games in Los Angeles. Victor Davis of
Canada (bottom of picture) went on to win the
silver medal.

CRESTWOOD HOUSE

Macmillan Publishing Company
866 Third Avenue
New York, NY 10022

Macmillan Publishing Company is part of the
Maxwell Communications Group of Companies

First published in Great Britain
in 1991 by Wayland (Publishers) Ltd
61 Western Road, Hove, East Sussex BN3 1JD

Printed in Italy by G. Canale & C.S.p.A.
1 2 3 4 5 6 7 8 9 10

ACKNOWLEDGMENTS

The Publisher would like to thank the
following agencies and photographers
for allowing their pictures to be
reproduced in this book: All Sport UK
Photographic Limited 4, 7, 9, 12, 13,
14, 15 (top), 17 (Tony Duffy), 19, 20, 22
(Simon Bruty), 23, 26 (top), 29 (Tony
Duffy), 30, 31 (Simon Bruty), 33 (Don
Morley), 35 (Tony Duffy), 40 (Ken
Levine), 42 (Tony Duffy), 44 (right,
Pascal Rondeau); Colorsport COVER, 5
(Zihnioglu), 6 (Paul J. Sutton), 7, 18, 21,
24, 25, 26 (bottom), 27, 28, 34, 36,
37, 38, 39 (both: top, Rick Rickman),
41 (both), 43, 44 (left), 45; Topham
Picture Library 10, 11, 15 (bottom), 16.

Library of Congress Cataloging-in-Publication Data

Sandelson, Robert
   Swimming and diving/Robert Sandelson.
      p.   cm. — (Olympic sports)
   Includes bibliographical references
    and index.
   Summary: An overview of the events that
make up the swimming and diving portion of the
Olympic Games, with highlights of great athletes
and moments.
    ISBN 0−89686−670−X
    1. Swimming — Juvenile literature. 2. Diving —
Juvenile literature. 3. Olympics — History
— Juvenile literature. [1. Olympics — History.
2. Swimming. 3. Diving.] I. Title. II. Series.
GV837.6.S25   1991
797.2'1 — dc20   91-16117

CONTENTS

THE OLYMPIC IDEAL

Swimming has become an increasingly fashionable sport. Because of the nature of the sport, both male and female swimmers have broad shoulders and well-developed bodies. They are often in demand as models. Also, because of the obsession with health and fitness in the 1990s, sports clothes have become very fashionable. Although swimwear designs seem fairly limited, the range of costumes is awesome. Those with designer labels are especially popular. Swimmers, with their shaved heads and multicolored lycra swimsuits, have helped to make the sport glamorous. This encourages increased participation. The Olympic Games provide a thrilling and exciting arena for the sport. Its stars receive media attention and are exposed to a worldwide television audience.

▲ Members of the Swedish women's relay team wearing fashionable, futuristic all-in-one lycra swimsuits.

Swimming and diving as sports have been around for thousands of years. But there is no evidence that they were part of the original Olympic Games held in ancient Greece. Swimming has been part of the modern Olympics since the first modern Games in Athens in 1896. Women, however, did not participate until the 1912 Stockholm Games.

Many swimming events have appeared and then quickly disappeared from the Olympic Games during its long history. These included the plunge for distance, underwater swimming and obstacle racing. The plunge for distance required the competitors to enter the pool from a standing dive and glide motionlessly underwater. The winner was the man who could go the furthest in 60 seconds or until his head broke the surface.

The first plunge competition was held at the 1904 Games in St. Louis. The winner was William Dickey of the

United States with a plunge of 62 feet 6 inches (approximately 19 m). However, the big stars of the plunge for distance did not compete in the St. Louis Games. British swimmer John Arthur Jarvis, for example, won the 1904 Amateur Swimming Association (ASA) title with a plunge of 75 feet 4 inches (approximately 23 m). Unfortunately for him, the event was not included in the 1908 London Games. He never won an Olympic medal.

The history of Olympic swimming and diving is filled with great names and breathtaking events. People such as Johnny Weissmuller, Dawn Fraser, Mark Spitz, Kornelia Ender, Klaus Dibiasi, and Greg Louganis have brought controversy, glamor, popularity and excellence to both sports. These athletes are valued members of the Olympic movement.

▼ The 1988 U.S. men's 4 × 200 m relay team celebrate their victory at the Seoul Olympics. Team members were Troy Dalbey, Matt Letlinski, Doug Gjertsen and Matt Biondi.

50-M FREESTYLE

The 50 m for men and women was first held at the Olympic level in Seoul in 1988. A similar sprint race over 50 yards (approximately 46 m) was held in St. Louis in 1904. The St. Louis Games were something of a disaster. They took place over an incredibly long period of time—four and a half months. It was generally thought that the Games had contained too many events, so some were dropped from the Athens Games in 1906.

The 50 m was added to the events in Seoul because of its popular appeal. Naturally enough, the first heats in both the men's and women's events produced new Olympic records. For the men, Matt Biondi of the United States broke the record and went into the final as the fastest qualifier with 22.39 seconds. Biondi stormed ahead almost immediately in the final and won the gold medal in 22.14 seconds. His great rival, Tom Jager, won the silver medal in 22.36 seconds. Jager, the world champion and pre-race favorite, said afterward: "I swam a good race, Matt swam a great race. That's the difference."

The fastest qualifier going into the women's final was Chinese swimmer Wenyi Yang. She had swum the race in 25.67 seconds. However, in the final the great star of the Games was Kristin Otto of East Germany. She led all the way to a gold medal and set an Olympic record time of 25.49 seconds. This was the brilliant Otto's sixth gold medal of the Seoul Games. Wenyi Yang could only improve her first round time by 0.03 seconds. She had to settle for second place and a silver medal.

▲ Tom Jager of the United States doing some breathing exercises before a race. Jager won the silver medal in the 50 m in Seoul. It was the first time the distance was swum at the Olympics.

▲ Teammates and good friends, Tom Jager (left) and Matt Biondi were rivals in the 50 m in Seoul in 1988.

▼ The swimming star of the 1988 Olympics, Kristin Otto. She won one of her six gold medals in the 50-m freestyle.

100-M FREESTYLE

Until the 1988 Games in Seoul, the 100 m was *the* sprint swim. The distance was first raced at the first modern Olympics in Athens in 1896. Competitors had to swim in the Bay of Zea, near Piraeus, in perilously cold water — 55°F (12°C). The ideal racing temperature is thought to be at least 76°F (24°C). Alfred Hajos emerged 100 m later as the winner in 1:22.2 minutes. The time was, as he said: "Nothing to brag about," but he did swim in conditions that no swimmer today would even think of. Hajos went on to win a dramatic victory in the 1500-m freestyle at the same Games.

In Athens, 1896 all the freestyle swimmers used the single arm side-stroke. Afterward the crawl style of swimming emerged as the fastest stroke. Various swimmers around the world had experimented with different styles to find out which was the fastest. The first swimmer to perfect what we now know as the front crawl was American Charlie Daniels. He won the 100 m at the London Games in 1908. By the end of his career, Daniels had won one silver, two bronze and five gold medals from various Olympic Games. Considering that in those days there were far fewer events, this was an achievement that ranks alongside that of Mark Spitz.

Women freestyle swimmers enjoyed the Olympic spotlight before female track and field athletes. The first women's Olympic 100-m race took place in Stockholm in 1912. It was won by Fanny Durack of Australia. Until recently Australian women swimmers have, unfortunately, been treated rather poorly by their country's officials. Fanny Durack was no exception. However, she won the gold medal in Stockholm despite this lack of support.

Two great names dominated the sprint events between 1912 and 1928: Duke Kahanamoku and Johnny Weissmuller. The two great swimmers were very glamorous figures. Both went on to become movie stars after their swimming careers were over. Duke, born in Honolulu, was named by his parents in honor of the Duke of Edinburgh, who happened to be visiting the nearby island of Hawaii at the time of his birth. Duke claimed to have learned the modern front crawl from other Hawaiians, who had been doing it for generations!

When he arrived in Stockholm for the 1912 Olympics, Duke was an immediate hit. He impressed the Europeans with his grace and strength in the water. His dominance in the 100m was amazing. In the final he was able to look back at the 50-m half-way mark to check his huge lead. At the next Games, in Antwerp in 1920 (the 1916 Games did not take place

because of World War I), the 30-year-old Duke was still in fine form. He equaled his own world record in the 100-m semifinal. Then in the final he broke it by a full second in 1:01.4 minutes. The Olympic Games were in Duke's blood and he could not retire. Incredibly, he competed in 1928 in Amsterdam and again in 1932 in Los Angeles, though he did not win individual medals at either Games.

Although the 1-minute barrier was constantly challenged by Duke, it took another superb swimmer to break through it—Johnny Weissmuller. In 1922, two years after Duke received his gold medal, Weissmuller became the first person to be timed at under 1 minute for the 100 m. Following this barrier-breaking swim of 59.6 seconds, he lowered the record again to 58.6 seconds. In the 1924 Olympic year he swam 57.4 seconds—a record that remained unbeaten for 10 years.

Weissmuller, born in Austria, was taken to the United States by his parents at the age of four. He was a weak, sickly child. However, the special exercises prescribed for him by doctors worked wonderfully. At the 1924 Games in Paris, Weissmuller displayed awesome skill and beat his rivals with ease.

◀ Johnny Weissmuller poses for photographers at the 1924 Games in Paris. Weissmuller won the 100-m freestyle in Paris and in Amsterdam in 1928.

Altogether at the Games, he won gold medals in the 100 m, 400 m and 4 × 200 m relay and a bronze in water polo. His popularity was increased by a comic diving act he put on for the delighted crowd. A hint perhaps of his future career? Four years later in Amsterdam in 1928, Weissmuller again displayed his world-class skills. He practically drowned when he swallowed a lot of water in the finals of the 100 m. However, he was able to recover and won the race by over 1 second in 58.6 seconds.

While in training for a third Olympics, the 1932 Los Angeles Games, Weissmuller turned professional. He accepted a contract to advertise a certain brand of swimwear. This began what was to be a lucrative second career. So he did go to Los Angeles in 1932, though as a movie star and not a swimmer. *Tarzan, The Ape Man* was released in the Olympic year. The sickly Austrian child, turned world-record-breaking swimmer, turned swimwear model, had become a Hollywood hero.

While Johnny Weissmuller was thrilling audiences at the Paris Games in 1924, another swimming star was emerging. The Games witnessed the first appearance of one of the most remarkable of all women swimmers — Gertrude Ederle of the United States. The daughter of a New York butcher, Ederle was beaten into third place in the 100-m and 400-m freestyle. These bronze medals turned out to be the least of Ederle's achievements. Two years later, having fallen in love with Europe during the Olympics, she returned to France and swam the English Channel. This feat shocked the world. Ederle's time was two hours faster than the men's record.

▼ Johnny Weissmuller with Maureen O'Sullivan in a scene from the Hollywood movie *Tarzan, The Ape Man.*

Dawn Fraser

Of all Olympic swimming champions the greatest was Dawn Fraser of Australia. She performed with a consistency that will probably never be seen again. She won three consecutive 100-m titles — a feat that is unmatched in the history of swimming. What is even more incredible is that her victories came in the event with the most competition of all. This is not to demean the achievements of athletes such as American Al Oerter who won the men's discus four times in a row. In a sport where people in their mid-twenties are considered over the hill, Fraser won her last gold medal at the grand old age of 27. She was also severely asthmatic.

The story of Dawn Fraser is one of an incredibly talented woman who did not conform to any expected feminine image and was grudgingly tolerated by

▲ New Yorker Gertrude Ederle swims the English Channel in 1926.

the authorities all her life. It was her asthma that first got her to the pool; the moist warm air was good for her lungs. She swam for hours each day and was soon beating everybody — a pattern that was to be repeated. At the age of 19 she broke the 20-year-old world record in the 100 m, as well as records in the 200 m and 200 yards. Her asthma prevented her from swimming longer distances.

Two years later, at the 1956 Olympics in Melbourne, Australia, Fraser took her first step toward sports immortality. In the 100 m, in front of a home crowd that included her parents, she beat her great rival Lorraine Crapp to take the gold medal. Her triumph was hard won and she became a hero in Australia.

Australian swimmer Dawn Fraser.

Over the next four years she had to work carefully to keep her amateur status. This meant giving up a university scholarship and keeping her job in a department store. In 1960, at the Rome Games, she was involved in a controversy over the butterfly event. Although Fraser was the world record holder, she had suffered bad side effects from swimming the butterfly. She had been told by her doctors to give it up. The authorities made her life a misery when she withdrew from the event. Fraser ignored them and took the 100-m freestyle title, refusing to let the unpleasant atmosphere rob her of a gold medal.

Two years later, Fraser reached a new peak when she became the first woman to swim the 100 m in under a minute. Then came the tragedy of her mother's death in a car crash, in which Fraser was also injured. This only temporarily affected her training program for the next Olympics in Tokyo in 1964. There, although troubled by a cold aggravated by asthma, she won again. A late-night prank saw Fraser banned by the Australian authorities. At the same time a more forgiving world cheered her brilliant triple victory.

She was awarded an MBE (Member of the British Empire) by the Queen. Banned from amateur status, she went to the Mexico Games in 1968 as a guest. She was a spectator when her title was taken with a slow time — surely a disappointing experience for a competitor of Fraser's ability. She held the 100-m freestyle record for a remarkable 16 years from 1956 until 1972.

Swimming is a sport that usually rewards its young stars for a very short time. In recent times the pressure on sprint swimmers has become even more intense. The sprint races are the glamor events. The competitors are expected to peak at exactly the right times. Swimming champions are also, on average, even younger than track athletes.

In this context the achievement of American Ambrose "Rowdy" Gaines deserves a special mention. Gaines was the world record holder in the 200 m prior to the 1980 Moscow Games. He consistently swam the fastest times in the world over 100 m. The Games were boycotted by the United States because of the Soviet invasion of Afghanistan. This meant that Gaines could not compete at these Olympics. For a modern swimmer the chances of winning another gold medal were highly unlikely.

Four years later in Los Angeles, the 25-year-old was being written off by everyone. He even started to believe his own critics. As the oldest member of the American team, Gaines could be forgiven for his doubts. His performance in the Olympic trials only served to further discourage him. He did not qualify for the 200 m and was pushed into second place in the 100 m. Fate was on his side, however. In the Olympic 100-m final, his toughest opponent, Australian Mark Stockwell, had a poor start and could not catch Gaines, who stormed to the finish — a winner against all the odds.

▼ American Rowdy Gaines won the 100 m in Los Angeles in 1984.

200-M FREESTYLE

The 200-m freestyle race was held in Paris in 1900, and St. Louis in 1904, but then not again until 1968 in Mexico City. The 1900 race was held in the Seine River. The swimmers were assisted by the current.

When the 200 m was held again, 64 years later, the winning time was achieved by Michael Wenden, a member of the excellent Australian swimming team. His time was 1:55.2 minutes — without a current!

The women's 200 m was first swum at the Olympics in Mexico City in 1968. One of the greatest women swimmers was Kornelia Ender. She was spotted at an early age by the efficient East German coaching system (now discontinued) and put into intensive training. At the 1972 Games in Munich, she won two silver medals at the tender age of thirteen. The East German team has been the dominant force in women's swimming since Dawn Fraser retired.

Between Munich and Montreal in 1976, the careful, scientific approach of the East German swimmers revolutionized swimming. They led in terms of medal-winning with the success of Ender. She broke the 100-m freestyle world record nine times between 1972 and 1976. However, Ender was not without challengers. Her greatest international rival was American Shirley Babashoff. In 1975, Babashoff beat her in the world championships in the 200 m. Ender's response was to later take 3 seconds

▲ Kornelia Ender spearheaded the phenomenal success of the East German swimming team in 1976. Here, she is pictured after winning the 200-m freestyle.

▲ Shirley Babashoff of the United States, Kornelia Ender's great rival in the 200-m freestyle at the Montreal Olympics in 1976.

▶ The superb Australian swimmer Shane Gould won the 200-m freestyle in 1972 in Munich.

off that winning time. By the time the Olympics came around in 1976, the competition seemed to be safely in Ender's hands. In the final, Babashoff went off quickly and stormed into the lead. Ominously, the superb East German closed in on her, meter by meter. By the third length (150 m) she had caught and passed the struggling Babashoff. Ender cruised home to an easy victory and an Olympic gold medal.

400-M FREESTYLE

I t is a remarkable fact that from 1920 until 1960, women swimmers were allowed to swim farther than women athletes were allowed to run (except for a single 800 m held at the Amsterdam Olympics in 1928).

The history of the 400-m freestyle began in 1896 with the birth of the modern Games. The first great women's Olympic 400-m champion was Martha Norelius. Born in Stockholm, she became an American citizen and could, therefore, compete for the United States. Her father had been an Olympic-class swimmer for Sweden. In Paris in 1924, Norelius made her first great win when she beat the world record holder, Gertrude Ederle, for the gold medal. Within two years she had managed to break the existing world record. She then went on to break it in the heats and in the final of the 1928 Games. Norelius became the first woman to win two successive Olympic titles. She lost her amateur status in controversial circumstances. She was accused of receiving payments for swimming with professionals. Although she always denied it, her career as an amateur was finished. With no other option, she became a professional.

The most famous swimmer turned actor after Johnny Weissmuller was Buster Crabbe. He won the 400-m Olympic title in 1932 in Los Angeles. In a close final the world record holder, Jean Taris of France, took an early lead. Crabbe slowly caught up.

Then, with the excited crowd out of their seats and practically in the pool with their local hero, he forged ahead in the last remaining strokes to win one of the most popular swimming victories. Later the champion cleverly remarked —after he had been signed up by Hollywood filmmakers—that the 0.1-second victory seemed to have an enormous effect on his acting skills! Crabbe, like Weissmuller, also played Tarzan. But he was best known for his portrayal of *Flash Gordon, Savior Of The Universe*. He was a hero to countless

▲ Buster Crabbe (right) as Flash Gordon.

American Janet Evans won the 400-m and 800-m freestyle races in Seoul in 1988.

children who thrilled to his adventures on movie screens around the world. Crabbe's place in swimming history is important because he developed the very high elbow recovery technique in the freestyle stroke. This technique is now commonplace in swimming. It results in less lateral (side to side) movement throughout the body and, therefore, less resistance.

The clash between Hendrika "Rie" Mastenbroek of the Netherlands and Ragnhild Hveger of Denmark at the 1936 Berlin Games was a real classic. The Berlin Olympic Games took place under the shadow of Nazi leader Adolf Hitler and his fascist supporters. The competitors had to perform while the threat of a potential world war was ever-present. The contrast between the later careers of the Dutch and Danish swimmers could hardly have been more extreme. But for those 5½ minutes while they battled against each other in the pool little could separate them. For Mastenbroek the

Games meant great Olympic glory. For Hveger it was the start of a career full of records but, because of World War II, no Olympic joy. Hveger finished fifth in the 400 m in Helsinki in 1952, but at the age of 31, she was past her prime.

Between 1938 and 1953, Hveger was the official world record holder in the 200 m, 400 m, 800 m and 1500 m. To become an Olympic champion, however, requires just that little bit more. It required something special that all the world records in history cannot quite equal. On the day of the 400-m final in 1936, Hveger went into the lead from the start and appeared comfortable until the 375-m mark. Then, showing true Olympian spirit and fight, Mastenbroek fought back. With only 25 m to go, the Dutch swimmer passed Hveger and went on to win the coveted gold medal.

800-M FREESTYLE

Not all the great swimmers can be Olympic champions. This has been proven time and time again in the history of the Games. In fact, the ''nearly'' or ''almost'' winners have often added great spice to the competition. If things always went as planned or people won by rights there would be nothing to make the Olympics special.

In the case of Shirley Babashoff of the United States, we cannot help but wish that just one race could be re-swum and she could win the individual gold she so longed for. A swimmer with movie star looks and ferocious dedication, she seemed destined always to come in second. In 1972, in Munich, she won two silver medals, in both the 100-m and 200-m freestyle finals. Refusing to quit, she came back to Montreal in 1976 in search of that elusive gold. As the world record holder in the 800 m, Babashoff withdrew from the 400-m individual medley to save her strength. (The medley is four lengths, 100 m each,

made up of the freestyle, backstroke, breaststroke and butterfly.) In the final, Petra Thuemer of East Germany, who was the former world record holder, beat Babashoff for the gold. Babashoff, however, was the ultimate competitor. Refusing to give up, she played a vital role in the 4 × 100 m relay to give the American women's swimming team their only gold medal of the Games.

▶ ▼ Petra Thuemer of East Germany (opposite) beat Shirley Babashoff (below) of the United States into the silver medal position in Montreal in 1976. Babashoff did not go home empty-handed. She won the gold in the 4 × 100 m relay.

1500-M FREESTYLE

The 1500 m is an extremely demanding race. It requires great skill, strength and ability. The race began with near fatalities in the cold and choppy waters off the coast of Greece in the 1896 Games. It was a terrifying ordeal for the competitors. Alfred Hajos, the victor in the 100-m race, covered himself with grease for protection against the freezing water. In the event, many of the others struggled and had to be rescued. Hajos, who claimed afterward to have thought more about surviving than Olympic glory, won the race almost 4 minutes in front of the only other finisher. Hajos's glory, however, did not go unrecognized. Fifty-six years after this race, he was awarded a special diploma in recognition of his service to the Olympic movement.

▲ Mike Burton wears his gold medal after victory in the 1500 m in 1972.

Kusuo Kitamura of Japan was only 14 years old when he won the 1500-m freestyle event at the Los Angeles Games in 1932. He was the youngest-ever swimming gold medalist. What was even more amazing was that Kitamura's time of 19:12.4 minutes was an Olympic record for 20 years.

The most remarkable swimming performances in this event, though, belong to Michael Burton of the United States and Victor Salnikov of the Soviet Union. Burton, born in Des Moines, Iowa, is the only swimmer to win this event in successive Olympic Games. His story is an extraordinary one. As a boy, Burton was involved in a terrible accident. It resulted in his having severed tendons under his right knee and a badly damaged hip. Doctors advised him to swim as treatment for his muscles. This instruction, like that prescribed for Dawn Fraser's asthma, had an important effect on his life. Burton held five world records in the

1500 m. The last came in the final in Munich in 1972 when he won the Olympic gold medal.

Salnikov proved himself a more than worthy successor to Burton in this event. Only the Montreal Games separated them. In 1980, in Moscow, he broke the greatest barrier in distance swimming by finishing the 1500 m in under 15 minutes. He did not compete in Los Angeles in 1984 because of the boycott. (None of the East European nations, except for Romania, attended the Games because of the United States' boycott of the 1980 Moscow Games.) No one came close to Salnikov's world record time of 14:54.76 minutes. He would surely have won in Los Angeles. Yet again, political interference in sports led to a great athlete being denied his moment of Olympic glory.

▲ Victor Salnikov of the Soviet Union was triumphant in the 1500 m in 1980 and 1988.

In the following years, and in the build-up to the next Olympics, Salnikov's form was disappointing. First, at the 1986 world championships, and then at the 1987 European championships, he showed a lack of desire to win. It looked more and more as if his Olympic career was over. But the greatest Olympians defy all logic. Salnikov stormed home to win the gold medal in the 1500 m in Seoul in 1988. The huge roar from the crowd included the raised voices of other swimmers from all nations. They appreciated and cheered his incredible dedication. They all knew what an amazing feat it was to be at the top, fall, and return again eight years later.

100-M BACKSTROKE

The backstroke was the third stroke, after the freestyle and the breaststroke, to be included in the Olympic program when it was recognized in 1908 in London. In the early years the backstroke was being altered constantly. One of the most important stylists was the American Adolph Keifer. In the Berlin Olympics in 1936, he showed the world his low arm recovery when he swam with wide, outstretched arms. Keifer won the 100-m gold medal. Since then, many other backstroke swimmers have imitated his style.

Women first competed in an Olympic 100-m backstroke in 1924 in Paris. Eighteen-year-old Aileen Riggin, best known as a diver, lined up in the final.

In the Antwerp Games in 1920 as a 14-year-old American schoolgirl, Riggin won the springboard diving gold medal. The competition in the backstroke event was very stiff. Riggin wanted desperately to win. No one had ever won medals in both swimming and diving events. Swimming against her was the world record holder, Sybil Bauer of the United States. The race went as planned, with Bauer winning by the huge margin of 4 seconds. Riggin came in third—good enough to win the medal she needed for a unique Olympic swimming record. Her feat has since been matched by only two other women and one man.

▼ The start of the 100-m backstroke final in Seoul in 1988.

The 1936 Berlin final was more famous for one spectator than all swimmers. She was Eleanor Holm. The Holm story starts in 1932 in Los Angeles when, as world record holder, she won the 100-m backstroke title. She turned down many offers from Hollywood producers. She wanted to remain an amateur and, therefore, be eligible for the Berlin Games. She set world records in the 100-m and 200-m backstrokes and was considered the favorite to retain her 100-m title. Unfortunately, in those days there was a long and, for the athletes, boring sea journey across the Atlantic. For the extremely independent and fun-loving Holm, the trip was too long. In her efforts to liven up the trip she became the unfortunate victim of the Olympic authorities. They criticized her for ruining the team's reputation after a champagne-filled evening. The stuffy president of the AOC (American Olympic Committee), Avery Brundage, saw to it that Eleanor Holm would not represent her country.

The backstroke style changed slowly after World War II. The greatest controversy came in Seoul in 1988 when Igor Polianski of the Soviet Union used what quickly became known as the "submarine start." This was first controversial in 1980 at the Moscow Games, where British swimmer Gary Abrahams used it. Many people believed Abrahams would have won the gold medal if he had not run out of oxygen during his start. Underwater swimming is faster than normal swimming. In the breaststroke there was so much use of underwater swimming that the rules were changed after 1956. The swimmers were required to keep their heads above the water. In the backstroke there was no such rule. Polianski pushed off and, using only his legs to propel himself, stayed completely under the water for the best part of the first 50 m.

▲ Igor Polianski of the Soviet Union was famous for his "submarine start." He used the tactic most successfully in the 200 m in Seoul in 1988, where he won the gold medal.

200-M BACKSTROKE

Men did not compete in an Olympic 200-m backstroke race between 1904 and 1960. Perhaps the greatest backstroker of all time was Roland Matthes. This East German first came to notice at the early age of only 16, when he set his first backstroke world record. He broke the records in the 100-m and 200-m backstroke 16 times by the age of 22. From April 1967, when he was beaten by fellow East German Joachim Rother, until August 1974, when he lost to John Naber, Matthes was undefeated in the 200-m backstroke.

He won golds in this event in Mexico City in 1968 and Munich in 1972. But for an emergency appendix operation, Matthes might have won a third consecutive gold in Montreal in 1976. He was very much a product of the East German sports machine, coached to a peak of mental as well as physical fitness. Matthes possessed the flexibility, height and agile approach to the stroke that made him known as the ''Rolls-Royce'' of backstroke swimming. He later married the famous woman swimmer Kornelia Ender.

The first women's Olympic 200-m backstroke took place in Mexico in 1968. The final featured perhaps the greatest backstroker never to win an Olympic gold.

Elaine Tanner was a Canadian with British parents. She was known as Canada's ''Mighty Mouse'' because of her 5 foot 2 inch (1.6 m) build. In the 1966 Commonwealth Games, she

◀ John Naber of the United States won the backstroke final at the Games in Montreal in 1976.

won four gold and three silver medals, breaking two world records in the process. In the following year at the Pan-American Games held in Winnipeg, Tanner won the 100-m and 200-m backstroke. Again she set new world records. Her times were slightly lowered by Karen Muir soon after. Muir, though, as a South African, was unable to compete in the Olympic Games. Her country was banned from competition because of its unacceptable system of racial apartheid. This left Tanner with a perfect opportunity to win an Olympic gold medal.

▲ East German swimmer Roland Matthes powers into the lead in the final of the 200-m backstroke in Munich in 1972. Matthes won the event in Munich and four years earlier in Mexico City.

However, the pressure of being such a strong favorite to win, and the high expectations of the public, took their toll on her performance. She felt unable to concentrate on the race. In the end it took an inspired swim from Kaye Hall of the United States to deny Tanner the gold medal. Hall's time was inside Karen Muir's world record. This made her a worthy winner indeed.

▲ Roland Matthes chats with a time-keeper in Munich in 1972.

▼ American Jesus Vassallo at the start of the 200-m backstroke final in Seoul in 1988.

100-M BREASTSTROKE

T he breaststroke has experienced many changes in style and technique in its long history. Over the years the definition of what exactly makes up a breaststroke has changed as the swimmers continually come up with new styles designed to give them an advantage over their opponents.

The most famous loopholes that the swimmers exploited were swimming underwater and bringing their arms *above* the surface of the water. In this last case, American swimmers practiced what we now refer to as the butterfly, which became an Olympic event in its own right in 1956.

Underwater swimming was developed by Japanese racers. It improved times so signficantly, and in such a short space, that a year after the Melbourne Olympics in 1957 the authorities changed the rules. From then on, except for the start of the race and the first stroke and kick after each turn, a part of the head *had* to be kept above the surface of the water. Women competed in Olympic 200-m breast-stroke races from 1924 onward. How-ever, it was not until Mexico City in 1968 that the shorter 100-m distance was added to the Olympic program. It was in this year that Djurdica Bjedov caused one of the biggest shocks in swimming in the history of the Olympic Games.

Bjedov did not have a particularly spectacular warm-up to the Olympics. Indeed, her third placing in the 1966 European championships had been her best performance ever. The lithe

▲ Duncan Goodhew continued the legacy of British Olympic breaststroke champions by winning the 100 m in Moscow.

student from Split was originally picked for the Yugoslavian team as a member of the relay squad. It was in this event that she hit rock bottom. As a result of her faulty takeover, the Yugoslavian team was disqualified and did not reach the final.

Things began to look up for Bjedov soon after. Her swimming began to improve. It seemed that she suffered less from the altitude in Mexico City than the other competitors. Due to an injury to another swimmer, Bjedov was chosen to step in and compete in the 100-m breaststroke. The Yugoslavian swimmer was given an opportunity to redeem herself. As the heats pro- gressed, she surprised everyone with her strong swimming. She qualified for the final with the fifth fastest time, which was far better than she expected. However, placed in slow lane two, Bjedov's Olympic challenge seemed to be over. But her form was world class, and she swam virtually unchallenged. She was also helped greatly by the fact that the world record holder, Catie Ball, was badly affected by a virus.

To show everyone that this was by no means a one-time performance, Bjedov went on to take the silver medal in the 200 m, again from an unfavorable outside lane. Her time was 3 seconds inside her personal best. Yet again, the mysterious ''Olympic effect'' had come into play. The record books had been turned upside down and an outsider took the title.

The men's 100-m breaststroke was first swum in the 1964 Rome Games. One of the most memorable wins in the event was by Duncan Goodhew of Great Britain in Moscow in 1980. (However, the race was without the American swimmers because of

▲ One of the proudest moments in Duncan Goodhew's life was receiving an Olympic gold medal for his victory in the 100-m breaststroke in Moscow in 1980.

the boycott.) Goodhew suffered from alopecia (chronic loss of hair) after falling out of a tree as a child. This condition left him bald, and at school he was teased by his peers because of this affliction. Perhaps the experience toughened his resolve to become a world-class athlete.

The American boycott of the Games had a considerable effect on Goodhew, both personally and professionally. His family was split by his participation. His stepfather, a retired air vice-marshal, refused to attend. His mother stood by her son. The lack of American swimmers prevented Goodhew from competing against the world's best swimmers. However, despite doubts and divisions, his victory was a very

▼ Adrian Moorhouse, one of the best known and most popular swimmers in recent years. His dedication and hard work has been an inspiration to young swimmers.

Another in the line of great British breaststroke swimmers, Adrian Moorhouse (left). He is on the blocks ready to go at the start of the 100-m breaststroke final in Seoul in 1988.

fine one. It was part of the revival for British breaststroke swimmers. In fact, another British swimmer, Adrian Moorhouse, dominated the breast-stroke throughout the 1980s.

Moorhouse made the 100-m final in Los Angeles in 1984. His swimming steadily improved and, although he had a disappointing result in the 1986 world championships, he was back to his best for the Seoul Games in 1988.

However, the fact that Moorhouse was at his best was not exactly obvious in the final. At the half-way mark he was in sixth place, and clearly looked beaten. Even 25 m from the end, a British medal looked unlikely. But, suddenly, the rest of the field seemed to be treading water. Moorhouse put on his finishing sprint and caught up with the leaders, winning with only 0.01 second to spare.

The story does not end there, however. Two years later, in 1990, Adrian Moorhouse still held the world record. No other swimmer had managed to beat him in the 100-m breaststroke. Although the experts claim that swimmers are supposed to peak in their early twenties, Adrian Moorhouse defied all the rule books. He is also the first person to swim the 100-m breaststroke in under a minute.

▼ Bulgarian swimmer Tania Dangalakova clasps her head in joy and disbelief after finishing in first place in the women's 100-m breaststroke final in Seoul in 1988. She beat some excellent rivals on her way to the gold medal.

200-M BREASTSTROKE

The 200-m breaststroke was the standard Olympic distance at the 1908 London Games. The great number of styles and changes of technique that have evolved since make a continuous history of the event extremely hard to outline.

Another change that distorts the history of the 200-m breaststroke was the banning of underwater swimming. Masaru Furukawa of Japan swam faster in the 1956 Games in Melbourne than the gold medalist in 1960 in Rome, and faster than some of the finalists in 1964! This is exceptional since the history of swimming has otherwise been one of steady improvement in times.

The next great leap forward was the change in the timing of the stroke. The swimmer took a breath at the end of the stroke rather than during. But, as so often happens in the Olympics, the innovators and world record holders are not always the medal winners. The swimmer who pioneered this stroke was Chester "Chet" Jastremski. He won a bronze in the 1964 Games in Tokyo, though in 1961 he had lowered the record by a phenomenal 6.9 seconds.

The history of the women's 200-m breaststroke follows, in technical respects, the history of the men's event. The use of the butterfly arms, the underwater stroking, and the resulting drop in the world record times, all occurred in the 1930s and 1950s. What is quite different is the young age of many female champion swimmers. The 1936 Games held in Berlin best illustrate this. The 200-m breaststroke bronze medalist was Inge Sorensen from Denmark. At 12 years old she was the youngest-ever Olympic medalist. Martha Geneger, the silver medalist, was 14. The winner, Hideko Maehata, the world record holder from Japan, was relatively old at 22.

Inge Sorensen went on to win gold medals in the Nordic championships in 1937 and the European championships in 1939. She also swam world record times on three occasions before World War II ended her career. As the war in Europe took thousands of young lives, sporting competitions ceased to be held. As a holder of 14 Danish records, Sorensen's fame still lasts in her home country. She remains something of a national heroine.

There have been several reasons given to explain the amazing success of young people in swimming. Swimmers in general are much younger than other athletes, and there are several reasons for this. Swimming requires less sheer brute strength and power, which can take years to develop. Young people also have a greater buoyancy than adults. Their

natural flexibility, too, is of great value in the loose, rangy movements required. Perhaps most significantly, young people present less frontal resistance and, therefore, suffer less from drag. This explains the success of young swimmers. But there are other reasons why many swimmers, and women in particular, rarely continue in the sport after their teens. The need to develop bigger muscles as the body grows has often been cited as the reason why women have dropped out

▲ The darling of British swimming in the 1960s, Anita Lonsbrough. She won the 200-m breaststroke gold medal at the Games in Rome in 1960.

of the sport. The effect of the chlorine —it streaks the hair green—has also been blamed.

One of the most popular winners of the 200 m was Britain's Anita Lonsbrough. She demonstrated a peculiar mixture of grit and calmness that delighted the Olympic crowd in 1960. Before the 200-m final started she was seen coolly polishing her nails. During the race, Lonsbrough allowed her fast-starting rival, Wiltrud Urselmann from Germany, to take the lead. But the British swimmer always kept her within sight. Lonsbrough waited until the last 25 m to sprint home for the gold medal. Both Lonsbrough and Urselmann swam inside the world record mark.

One of the most memorable contests in the men's 200-m breaststroke was between David Wilkie, a Scotsman, and John Hencken of the United States. Wilkie was the silver medalist at the Munich Games in 1972, while Hencken took the gold. Over the next four years, however, Wilkie established his dominance in the event. Hencken, meanwhile, concentrated on the 100-m breaststroke. There was much discussion and debate about the rivalry between the two great swimmers. There was also intense speculation concerning their supposed dislike of each other. This was perhaps caused by the fact that in all the years they competed they never exchanged

▼ David Wilkie (center) proudly sporting his gold medal on the winner's podium after victory in the 200-m breaststroke in Montreal in 1976.

▲ David Wilkie powers through the water in Montreal in 1976.

more than an occasional word. The longest thing Wilkie can remember saying to Hencken was in the pool at the end of the 200-m breaststroke final in Montreal in 1976: ''John, it's been a good four years— thanks a lot.''

Prior to the final, Wilkie had been advised by his coach to make a fast start and then settle just behind Hencken. The Scotsman was then to lengthen his stroke while biding his time. Wilkie followed these instructions to perfection. At the turn into the third length, he was 0.4 second behind the American. It was at this point that Wilkie began his push, and Hencken was left behind. He finished in the record-shattering time of 2:15.11 minutes (3 seconds inside Hencken's world record). Wilkie was the first British male to win an Olympic swimming event in 68 years. He also held another unique record—he was the only male gold medalist in swimming at the Montreal Games who was not from the United States.

100-M BUTTERFLY

The butterfly developed as a separate and distinct stroke from the breaststroke when it was given Olympic status in 1956 at the Melbourne Games. At these Games a 200-m butterfly race was held, and 12 years later in Mexico, the 100-m butterfly was added to the program. It is a graceful stroke but the grace is hard-won. Swimmers consider it the most physically demanding of all the strokes.

The 100-m butterfly final in Mexico in 1968 featured one of the many disappointments Mark Spitz was to have at these Games. He was beaten in the final by his fellow American Doug Russell, something that had never occurred before. Spitz had won every other encounter between the two. Four years later, at the Munich Games, Spitz came back and set an Olympic record that stood for an unprecedented 12 years.

Unfortunately, the Munich Games were host to the worst tragedy in the history of the Olympics. The security of the Olympic village was broken by Palestinian terrorists who murdered two Israeli athletes in their dormitory, kidnapped nine more and killed them when police marksmen attempted to free the hostages. These events

▼ Michael Gross won the 100-m and 200-m butterfly races in Los Angeles in 1984.

▲ French swimmer Catherine Plewinski in the 100-m final in Seoul in 1988.

immediately changed the nature of the Olympics. For once national protests and rivalries were forgotten as the world mourned this tragedy. The atmosphere in which the Games continued was distinctly quiet. The brutality of what had happened made many want to halt the competition. The Games continued, however, but with little enthusiasm.

Mark Spitz was one of the outstanding features of the 1972 Munich Games. His 100-m butterfly record was broken in Los Angeles by Michael Gross of West Germany. Spitz's oustanding performance in the pool, where he won seven gold medals, places him alongside the all-time great Olympians. He was an inspiration to millions of young swimmers.

One of the biggest upsets of the Tokyo Olympic Games in 1964 was the victory by Sharon Stouder of the United States over Ada Kok of the Netherlands. Kok was the favorite but Stouder swam a magnificent race to beat her. She broke Kok's world record in the process.

Stouder had a marvelous Games. She participated in one of the greatest finals ever seen at any Olympics, when she came second to Dawn Fraser in the 100-m freestyle. In this race, when the Australian Fraser picked up her third consecutive gold in the event, Stouder became only the second woman to break the minute barrier.

200-M BUTTERFLY

For Ada Kok the disappointment of losing the 100-m butterfly in Tokyo to Sharon Stouder lasted until the following Games in Mexico City in 1968. Her world records in both the 100-m and 200-m butterfly events had not been turned into Olympic gold medals.

In the 100-m butterfly in Mexico, Ada Kok finished a disappointing fourth. Three days later she was standing on the blocks at the start of a 200-m final. She knew that this was probably her last appearance at an Olympic Games. Ada Kok, known as "The Gentle Giant," was the fastest qualifier and was not going to let this chance slip. True to form, her strong finish took her ahead, and in her last final, she won a coveted gold medal.

Mark Spitz

The 200-m butterfly marked the turning point in the swimming career of the greatest post-war swimmer of them all: Mark Spitz.

The story of Spitz is the story of a superior athlete and competitor. He overcame very human failings of pride and overconfidence and the prejudices of others to return to the Olympic

 The superb Mark Spitz.

stage and win seven gold medals in a single Games—an unrivaled performance. This is a record number of golds in any sport at a single Games, beating Nadi, the fencer who won five at Antwerp in 1920.

Spitz exploded onto the scene with five gold medals in the 1967 Pan-American games. He went to the Olympics in Mexico in 1968 as the outspoken favorite, claiming he would win six golds almost as if they were his

▶ Mark Spitz at practice in the UCLA swimming pool in Los Angeles.

▼ Mark Spitz finishes in his usual first place in Munich in 1972.

by right. But his performances were all below par, especially in the 200-m butterfly. The race came at the end of the swimming program in Mexico City. Spitz had qualified for the final with the best time. He was the world record holder in this event; however, the setbacks and the failure to win a gold medal by then had greatly depressed him. In the event, Spitz finished last in a field of eight, a humiliation that he would never again come close to repeating.

He returned to the United States to train with one of the world's great swimming coaches, named ''Doc'' Counsilman, at the University of Indiana. Spitz recovered the fitness and mental control that athletes need to compete at the highest level.

▼ Winner of an amazing seven gold medals at the 1972 Munich Olympics, Mark Spitz. He is photographed here in training in Los Angeles for a comeback appearance at the 1992 Games in Barcelona.

Four years later in Munich, Spitz stepped onto the blocks for the first swimming final of the Games, the 200-m butterfly. He was able to erase immediately the memory of four years before. He won in a world record time. It was the first of seven world-beating performances, and establishes Spitz's place in Olympic history.

► Michael Gross is known as ''The Albatross'' because of his enormous arm span. Gross was one of the stars of the 1984 Games in Los Angeles. He won gold medals in both the 100-m and 200-m butterfly.

▼ Brian Brinkley of Great Britain powers through the Olympic pool in Montreal in 1976 in the final of the 200-m butterfly.

DIVING

No one has ever dominated an Olympic event as Klaus Dibiasi of Italy dominated the highboard. His father, Karl, who had been a finalist in the 1936 Games in Berlin, was a remarkable diver and consistent athlete. He won his last Italian championship in 1962 at the age of 52. The following year, his son Klaus became the new world champion.

Karl, the proud father, took the 17-year-old to the Tokyo Olympics in 1964, and saw him win the silver medal. Dibiasi's losing margin was so small that he and his father returned to Italy with high hopes and expectations for Mexico City in 1968. The people of his home town, Bolzano, built him an indoor diving pool so he could practice all year round. Their generosity was rewarded when Dibiasi became Italy's greatest Olympic medal winner.

He won the gold in Mexico City in 1968, Munich in 1972, and Montreal in 1976. In the last of these tournaments, the young American Gregory Louganis posed something of a threat to the Italian. But Dibiasi, suffering from tendonitis in both heels, produced a stunning triple twist with one and a half somersaults. Dibiasi had his medals, and Louganis, the young contender, would have to wait a bit longer for his glory days.

▶ One of the greatest highboard divers in the history of the Olympics, Italian Klaus Dibiasi. He won three gold medals in consecutive Games: Mexico City in 1968; Munich in 1972; and Montreal in 1976.

Louganis was only 16 when he competed in that great final in Montreal. He had to wait longer than Dibiasi to get the satisfaction of stepping onto the winner's podium. Because of the American boycott of the Moscow Games, he did not compete in another Olympic final for eight years. In 1984, in his home town of Los Angeles, he took the gold medal in front of an adoring crowd. To add to this, Louganis also won the springboard. Four years later in Seoul in 1988, he retained both titles. Winning in Seoul was by no means easy for Louganis. Like Dibiasi before him, he learned that it never gets easier. In the qualifying rounds, he hit his head on the springboard as he came out of his third somersault. It was a shocking experience, and Louganis needed five stitches to close a nasty head wound. His determination and bravery were unwavering, however. When he came out of the hospital he took his place in the final and went on to win another gold medal.

At the opening ceremony for the 1984 Olympic Games in Los Angeles, the bearer of the Olympic flag was Pat McCormick. She represented America's finest Olympic champions. Born Pat Keller in California in 1930, she went to her first Olympic Games in Helsinki in 1952. There, she won both the platform and the springboard gold medals. She continued to train, even through pregnancy, and went to the Melbourne Games in 1956, to win

▲ China has consistently produced top-class divers. In Seoul in 1988 the tradition was carried on by Xu Yanmei, who won gold in the platform competition.

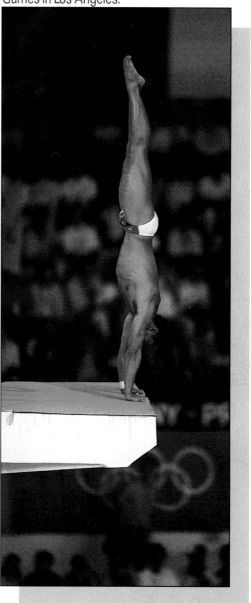

Greg Louganis competing in the 1984 Games in Los Angeles.

the two gold medals again. Her son was born only five months before the Games. Not only that, but McCormick's winning margin was the greatest ever recorded in Olympic competition. In 1965, she became one of the first women to enter America's Swimming Hall Of Fame.

Ingrid Engel-Kramer was another great competitor in the tradition of Olympic diving. She competed in three Games altogether. In 1960 in Rome, she became the first non-American to win the springboard while completing the double with a victory in the highboard.

▲ Louganis makes a perfect start to a dive in the 1988 platform final in Seoul.

▶ Greg Louganis flies through the air in Seoul in 1988.

GLOSSARY

Accolade Strong praise or approval.

Apartheid A racist system in a country where people of different races are kept apart and made to live in different areas and go to different schools.

Asthma An illness that affects the lungs and makes breathing difficult.

Boycott To refuse to do something or to stay away from somewhere in order to make a protest.

Commonwealth An organization of states that are, or at some time have been, ruled by Great Britain.

Controversy Something that is likely to cause an argument.

Definition An explanation of the exact meaning of something.

Eligible Someone who is worthy or qualified to do something.

Exponent Someone who demonstrates a particular skill.

Fascism The view held by Adolf Hitler that the Aryan race was superior to other races, especially Jews and blacks. In order to maintain his fascist system, Hitler aimed to control everything in Germany and to suppress all public criticism or opposition.

Flexible Easy to bend.

Ominous Suggesting future trouble and danger.

Prohibit To forbid or prevent someone from doing something.

Prolific Constantly producing results.

FURTHER READING

Frommer, Harvey. *Olympic Controversies.* New York: Franklin Watts, 1987.

Glubock, Shirley, and Alfred Tamarin. *Olympic Games in Ancient Greece.* New York: Harper Junior Books, 1976.

Greenberg, Stan, ed. *The Guinness Book of Olympic Facts & Feats.* New York: Bantam, 1984.

Marshall, Nancy Thies. *Women Who Compete.* Old Tappan, N.J.: Fleming H. Revell Company, 1988.

Tatlow, Peter. *The Olympics.* New York: Franklin Watts, 1988.

Walczewski, Michael. *The Olympic Fun Fact Book.* New York: Dell, 1988.

Wallechinsky, David. *The Complete Book of the Olympics.* New York: Penguin Books, 1988.

INDEX